16-18

THE ' JENKE ' PORTRAIT

This photograph was taken after the portrait had been cleaned
in the summer of 1950.

SCHOOL OF BACH-PLAYING
FOR THE ORGANIST

General Editor : GORDON PHILLIPS

VOLUME THREE

SCHOOL OF BACH-PLAYING FOR THE ORGANIST

General Editor: GORDON PHILLIPS

VOLUME THREE

Tempo and Rhythm
in
Bach's Organ Music

by
ROBERT DONINGTON

HINRICHSEN EDITION LTD.

Bach House, 10-12 Baches Street
London, N.1

373 Park Avenue South
New York 16, N.Y.

SOLE AGENTS:
C. F. PETERS CORPORATION
373 Park Avenue South
New York, N. Y. 10016

Printed in England by
ROBERT STOCKWELL LTD., LONDON, S.E.1

CONTENTS

MUSICAL EXAMPLES

Ex. 1

bar 13, as written

Ex. 2
as conventionally performed

Ex. 3

bar 16, as written   as conventionally performed   etc.

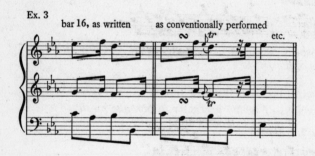

Ex. 4

bar 29, as written   as conventionally performed

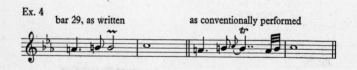

Ex. 5

bar 40, as written   as conventionally performed   etc.

6

MUSICAL EXAMPLES

Ex. 6 bar 57, as written   as conventionally performed

Ex. 7 as written

with *lourer*

(approximately)

Ex. 9 bar 7, as written   as conventionally performed

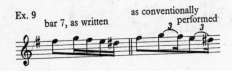

Ex. 10 bar 15, as written   as conventionally performed

7

MUSICAL EXAMPLES

Ex. 11

bars 90-91, as written

Ex. 12

bars 90-91, as conventionally performed

FOREWORD

IN THIS BOOK, which may be described as both unique and indispensable, the author brings his great learning to bear upon the problem of suitable tempo and rhythm in the performance of the Organ Works of J. S. Bach. This is a practical problem and Mr. Robert Donington deals with it in an eminently practical fashion. Such is the light thrown upon this specially tricky subject that I feel confident in asserting that every organist who wishes to perform J. S. Bach's works with anything approaching historical accuracy must needs read this book, not once but many times. Not only will the reader find each chapter a stimulating and exciting step further along the road to complete mastery, but at every turn he will find Mr. Donington at hand, ready with utterly practical advice; with, here and there, the necessary warning; and with an emphasis on individual musicianship so often lacking in other writers.

A thorny path must be trodden by all who wish to attain the stamp of authenticity in their performance. Mr. Donington must indeed be warmly congratulated on having provided this invaluable guide to the choice of route and the mode of travel.

GORDON PHILLIPS

9

CHAPTER ONE

TEMPO AS A PERFORMER'S RESPONSIBILITY

Why the right tempo is always a relative matter

ON the subject of tempo, J. S. Bach made the following comments in person, or almost certainly in person. They are part of a manuscript entitled " Instructions and rules for the playing of a Thorough-Bass . . . by Master John Sebastian Bach, Royal Court Composer . . . , for the use of his scholars in Music. 1738." The handwriting is that of one of these scholars of J. S. Bach, namely Johann Peter Kellner, and shows signs of having been taken at dictation either in this copy or in a previous original. There are mistakes in the music examples, but the following passage is clear enough; nor is there any real ground for doubting that it summarises the actual teaching of the master:

OF TIME OR MEASUREMENT

" Of this much need not here be said, for it is presupposed that a person wishing to learn figured-bass will not only have learnt the notes but also the intervals before doing so, whether by previous practice of music or from some other cause, and also the differences of time. For no one can inculcate a knowledge of time all at once. This must, however, be noticed, that in the present day one single kind of time is indicated in two ways, thus: C, 2;

the second way being used by the French in pieces that are to be played quickly or briskly, and the Germans and Italians adopting it from the French. But the Germans and Italians abide for the most part by the first method, and adopt a slow time. If the piece is to be played fast the composer expressly adds *Allegro* or *Presto* to it; if slowly, the pace is indicated by the word *Adagio* or *Lento* ".*

---

* The treatise is printed in full by Spitta, *Life of Bach*, English translation by Clara Bell and J. A. Fuller-Maitland, London, 1884-5, Vol. III, Appendix B, pp. 315-47. Characteristically, Bach saw no reason to be original where existing sources would serve; the treatise is largely pirated from F. E. Niedt's *Musical Handbook* of 1700.

And that, believe it or not, is all. No music examples; no systematic exposition of time-signatures; no attempt to define, or even to grade in order of speed, the few time-words mentioned. Nothing beyond a perfunctory warning that " a knowledge of time " is a difficult matter needing experience to acquire; and the revealing comment that C and 2 have come to mean one kind of time, with ₵ as an alternative to 2 not even mentioned, and the tempo-meanings left realistically vague.

Yet the excellence of Bach's teaching is attested by several of his pupils, and is not in doubt. The inference is unmistakable: J. S. Bach saw no useful purpose in listing detailed instructions; not because tempo is not important, but because it cannot be tied down to rules and measurements.

Composers as contrasted as Mozart and Wagner have insisted on the primary importance of hitting off the tempo (it was Wagner's test of a good conductor). Beethoven used Maelzel's newly popularised metronome most persistently—but it is also related that he became so bewildered by his own metronome markings on returning to them at a later date that he thought, quite unjustly, that his metronome must be at fault.

We have here the clue to this paradoxical mystery whereby tempo is everywhere admitted to be of the first importance, but nowhere satisfactorily defined or measured. The clue is that tempo is itself not a fixed quantity. The right tempo for a given piece of music is the tempo which fits, as the hand fits the glove, the interpretation of that piece *then being given* by the performer.

But as hands are of different sizes, so interpretations are in different moods. This is as it should be. An interpretation is always a combination of two people's visions: the composer's and the performer's. Provided that he is in fundamental sympathy with the music, the performer can enrich it from the storehouse of his own personality, and the stronger his personality, the more he can enrich it. No two performers, however, have the same personality, and no two performances even from the same performer will be quite alike. This fact is basic to all interpretation, and was as clearly understood in Bach's day as it is at present. We may confirm this from Bach's contemporary Quantz, one of the great teachers of his time and invaluable as a source of light on Bach's own practices.

" It would be too long and at times impossible, to give demonstrative proofs on matters which nearly always look only to taste . . . Some like what is majestic and lively, and others what is tender and gay . . . one is not always in the same mood."

(*Joachim Quantz, Essay, 1752, Preface and XVIII, 6-7*).

As the mood varies, so does the tempo which is right for that given occasion. Indeed, the limits within which the right tempo for any particular piece of music may vary are surprisingly wide. Yet the limits within which it can vary in the circumstances of any given occasion are narrow in the extreme. A very small deviation will give the listener a sense of discomfort. The reason is not that there is an absolute tempo which is right under all circumstances and which is being departed from—there is no such thing as an absolute right tempo; the reason is that the tempo no longer fits the given circumstances.

Here lies the paradox. What Beethoven had forgotten to allow for, when he unjustly blamed his metronome, was that the tempo he knew to be right on one occasion, and which he correctly wrote down as a metronome number, was not necessarily going to be right on another occasion. On the contrary, he later found it to be wrong; hence his suspicion and bewilderment.

The moral of this, namely that right tempo is a relative and not an absolute quantity, is the chief fact about tempo that a musician has to learn. Metronome markings are not, of course, to be despised. They give an exact tempo record as no other method does, and this record can be very useful as a starting-point and a point of comparison. But that is all. They can never decide the tempo on any given occasion; they can only give the most tentative of hints. That is, perhaps, why Bach himself, like the other composers of his time, made no use of them, although the principle on which the metronome is based was enunciated by Galilei over a century earlier, and practical applications of it had been discussed and used well before Bach was born. We begin to see now why his own tempo instructions are so brief and inexplicit. He knew, and we must clearly realise, that tempo is basically the responsibility of the performer.

Mood as a factor in the choice of tempo

We human beings are so profoundly variable in our fleeting shifts of mood that when we are in one mood we find it very hard to believe that we ever were or will be in any other—or even that anybody else can be either. This fact is of immense importance in determining not merely our preferences in music but also our interpretations.

That is perhaps fairly obvious when we come to think of it. What is not quite so obvious is that the music in which our moods are so richly expressed is itself capable of showing different faces to the world. It may be that shallow music, especially the commercialised music of Tin Pan Alley, can mean only one thing, and that of no very serious interest; but a composition of any lasting worth is not like that. However surprisingly, it is a matter of simple experience that the greatest classics are the most open to a variety of interpretations. This variety can be abused, but it genuinely exists, and different interpreters are able to show aspects of the music which we had not previously experienced. It is for this reason that the classics bear repeated hearing; and it is a dull interpreter who sees nothing in them but what others have seen before him. That is, after all, why interpretation is not mere reproduction but a creative art in which the performer's own personality as well as the composer's can find expression.

It will readily be appreciated that there are interpretations so intense and full of rich significance as to impose the slowest tempo within the outside implications of the music; and others so mercurial as to demand the fastest tempo within the possibilities of the case. These outside tempos may be quite considerably different, and yet each can be right in the particular circumstances at issue.

Acoustics as a factor in the choice of tempo

Sound in an enclosed space is partly absorbed, partly reflected. The part of it which is reflected may be reflected not once but many times. Arriving at the ear by longer routes than the sound which reaches us in a direct line, this reflected sound arrives at different times, all to some extent later than the direct sound. Hence the confusion which can reach troublesome proportions in buildings of which the reflecting capacity, or resonance, is excessive. The technical term for this confusion is reverberation.

Every musician is aware, and none better than the organist, how widely do different buildings vary in their reverberation. But it must not be imagined that reverberation in itself is hostile to musical performance; on the contrary, too little resonance is at least as undesirable as too much.

Sound in an enclosed space starts by building up energy faster than it is absorbed, until a balance is struck, which dwindles again after the source of sound falls silent. In an unusually absorptive building, the build-up takes longer, and gives the performer more sense of effort, besides being more difficult to maintain. In an unusually resonant building, the build-up comes quicker and is easier to maintain, giving the performer a sense of ease and well-being. But whereas in the first case there is so little reverberation that everything is stark-clear, in the second case there is so much reverberation that the music grows very confused indeed, every sound being reflected and heard many times over before its echoes finally die out. In the first case the music sounds unpleasantly dry; in the second, unpleasantly obscure.

On the basis of experience, the ideal reverberation time between the origin of the sound and the decay of its last appreciable echoes ranges from about one second for a small building to about two seconds for a large building. Where these conditions obtain, there is no necessity for the performer to modify his natural choice of tempo in deference to the prevailing acoustic situation. Where they do not obtain (and this is one of those ideals more honoured in the breach than in the observance) he will be very unwise indeed if he does not do so. For the less resonant instruments, it is usually enough that the instrumentalists respond to the prevailing acoustic conditions without being particularly aware of doing so. For any instrument so capable of power as the organ, it will be as well to consider the appropriate adaptation deliberately.

Where the building has a reverberation time shorter than the ideal, a rather quicker tempo can help to overcome the effect of dryness. Where the building has a reverberation time longer than the ideal (and it is this aspect of the problem with which, in the great majority of cases, organists have to contend), a rather slower tempo can help to lessen the confusion. And though this may sound a somewhat cold-blooded way of looking at the matter, it is not really so. Any organist worth his salt is accustomed to adapting his rendering, not only in tempo but in dynamics, registration, articulation and phrasing, to the building and indeed the organ in question, and is aware that the tempo which is thus sensitively adapted to the prevailing conditions is the tempo which will not only get over best to his audience, but will feel to himself most convincing musically. Or rather, it will do so provided he has acquired the art of judging his performance as it takes effect in the building as a whole and not merely in the organ-loft. But this, of course, is part of a good organist's skill in any case.

On the need to use well the few clues available

From what has been said above, it will be abundantly clear that any hints which we can obtain from Bach's original time-signatures and other tempo indications, or from the instructions given in the musical treatises of his time, can in the nature of the case only be of general assistance at the best. Moreover (and indeed perhaps for that very reason) these time-signatures and tempo indications prove on examination to be most casually and inconsistently applied, and the contemporary instructions prove to be highly contradictory with one another.

This casual inconsistency is extremely characteristic of the methods of writing music down which still prevailed in the time of Bach. It must not be inferred, however, that the composers of the day were indifferent to the many details of performance which they left so much vaguer in their notation than we attempt to render them at the present time. On the contrary, they paid as much attention to them as we do ourselves. The difference was that they preferred to leave within the province of the performer many elements which we expect to have decided for us at least in broad outline by the composer. This had nothing to do with either laziness or incompetence; it was a deliberate act of faith in the principle of individualism as applied to the interpretation of music. An age which still left the filling in of keyboard accompaniments and in most slow movements much of the ornamental figuration of the melody to be more or less improvised by the performer, was obviously determined to trust him with as much as possible, rather than like ourselves, with as little.   There were drawbacks to the system, but it was certainly an encouragement to spontaneous musicianship.

Tempo is an aspect of expression over which it is particularly difficult for the composer to help the performer.   Thus, in a system which left far more to the performer even than the very great amount which we are always compelled to do, we need not be surprised to find that more often than not Bach did not even trouble to write a tempo word such as *allegro* or *adagio* at the head of a piece, nor that his use of time-signatures often varies with no apparent reason and without effect on the musical results intended.   Nevertheless, the very fact that the clues are both slender and infrequent, so far from tempting us to ignore them, should encourage us to make the most careful study of what little direct evidence we have.   In the following pages, Bach's notation and the musical results which, in the light both of common sense and of the evidence of his own contemporaries, we can be reasonably certain that he intended, will be compared side by side.

There is one such piece of contemporary evidence which we may best consider here, by the side of Bach's own statement with which this chapter opened.   It is at one further remove from the master himself; but it is specifically concerned with his practice in performance, whereas the evidence later to be adduced is concerned only generally with the practice of his age.   It occurs in a notice of J. S. Bach contributed by his son, C. P. E. Bach and Agricola to a musical periodical shortly after the master's death:

> " J. S. Bach was very accurate in his conducting and very sure of his tempo which he usually took very lively." (*Mizler's Musikalische Bibliothek, V, iii: " Monument of three late members of the society of musical science* ").

This confirms, of course, that whereas J. S. Bach's own statement on tempo is brief and uninformative, his actual command of tempo was sure and clear.   There is nothing surprising in that.   We also learn that his choice of tempo struck at least some contemporary observers as on the lively side.   We must note the fact, but we must not exaggerate its importance.   We do not know what speed would have struck them as lively and what as sluggish. The hint is vague enough. It is valuable to know that we need not feel inhibited in giving Bach plenty of vivacity and brilliance where that is what the music itself implies. Yet in discovering these implications we are still brought back to where we started from: our own intuitive judgment and musicianship. That is the basis of expression, and not least in the matter of tempo. The evidence which follows deserves to be carefully weighed, but when it has been weighed the responsibility returns squarely to the performers, where it belongs.

CHAPTER TWO

TIME-SIGNATURES

All time-signatures the relics of an abandoned system

THE period of music which we loosely but conveniently call baroque, and of which J. S. Bach's lifetime occupied the closing portion, inherited from the Renaissance the fragmentary relics of a system of notation substantially different from its own. This previous system is sometimes called the proportional system, because the time-value allotted to different values of note in proportion to one another was not constant, but was governed by a series of highly complicated rules. The proportional system was the sum-total of these rules.

The method behind the proportional system of notating time-values may be most readily grasped by considering a few relics of it which survive in regular use to the present day. If in ordinary common time, four crotchets to the bar, we wish to introduce into the crotchet beat, let us say, notes not of half that beat's value (which would be straight quavers) but one-third, i.e. triplets, we do not call on a note-symbol indicative of that one-third time-value, for we have no such note-symbol to call on. There is no logical reason why we should not have; but instead, we indicate our intention in the manner of the old proportional system. We write quavers; but we say, in effect, " let these particular quavers bear the proportion not of two quavers to one crotchet but of three quavers to one crotchet". To help the performer, who may be reading at sight, we usually write a small three against the group as a safeguard against any possible ambiguity. But even if there is no written three, the proportion is the same, and will be seen to be so by an alert player with no particular difficulty.

Imagine this procedure carried to such lengths that every note-symbol in a complex composition may carry a variety of time-values in proportion to those of longer value, and you have the basis of proportional notation. Our familiar dot, giving half as much value again to the time-duration, is only one of many supplementary signs employed in proportional notation as an aid (a much-needed aid in all but the simplest instances) in reading the composer's intentions correctly. Indeed, our modern meaning of the dot is only one of several which this sign then bore. There were other indications of a similar order, such as the use of colour or the blacking-in or leaving white of the note-symbol itself. Above all, there was a very extensive series indeed of signs placed at the beginning of the performer's part to tell him what proportion his note-values were supposed to bear to the note-values given to the identical note-symbols in the other parts.

It is these signs which were the origin of our familiar time-signatures today. There were circles crossed with a stroke or with a dot in the middle; there were circles with no stroke or dot. There were circles cut in half to indicate a sub-division of the time—whence our common-time signature C (which is not, as it might seem to English musicians, the first letter of the word common, useful though this coincidence may be for mnemonic purposes!). There were half circles crossed by an upright stroke to indicate a further sub-division of the time—whence our $\mathbb{C}$. There were half circles with two, three, or even more upright strokes. There were other half-circles similar, but reversed to open towards the left instead of towards the right, again as a sign of sub-division. There were also various numerals, alone or in combination, such as our own $\frac{4}{4}$, $\frac{3}{4}$ etc. —but considerably more prolific and, to say the least of it, less self-explanatory.

The difficulties of such a system strike us today as highly formidable. They would be so, even granted the greatest consistency and order in their application. In fact, consistency and order could hardly have been more conspicuously lacking. The rules as we read them in the treatises of the time are often obscure enough, nor are the rules the same in different treatises. The whole system would have been unworkable but for one redeeming factor: tradition. Nothing is more obvious than the fact that oral teaching was the real foundation of the art. Notation was still quite largely what it had almost entirely been in its origins: more a reminder than a fully explicit text. In music even of the late Renaissance, the task of an editor preparing a text from which a modern performer can operate at all is often a task of great difficulty and skill.*

This is no longer so to any comparable extent by the seventeenth century, when the baroque styles of music were becoming gradually established. Many problems remain, but they are decidedly less formidable. And this is precisely the situation with regard to the problem of time-values. Basically, the system becomes the relatively straight-forward system to which we are now accustomed. The difficulties which do remain result from the fact that the old system did not vanish without trace, but left a number of somewhat bewildering inconsistencies behind it. By the time we reach the work of J. S. Bach, these inconsistencies were rather in the manner of writing music down than in the manner of performing it. Nevertheless, we need to know the answers if we are not to be confused; and indeed, even at so comparatively late a date in the history of notation as this, there are still a few inconsistencies of substance as well as of form.

Duple and Triple the only basic times

The main point to grasp with regard to old-fashioned time-signatures in J. S. Bach's music is precisely this point that they were not merely in essence obsolete by that date, but had been so already for some considerable time. By this I mean that the whole range of circles, half-circles, crossed circles or half-circles and so forth was in essence obsolete, since the system of proportional notation to which it related had been almost entirely abandoned in favour of the more simple (not wholly simple) arrangements with which we are now familiar. Consequently the manner of their use, frequent though it still was, had lost its basic significance. I do not mean that composers had no significance in mind when using them; but I do mean that the confusion which had by now arisen as to what that significance might really be had gone to such lengths that it is only our native intelligence and the more or less obvious implications of the music itself which can do very much to help us.

---

* The reader wishing to make a first-hand acquaintance with the mysteries of proportional notation could not do better than turn to Morley's *Plaine and Easie Introduction to Practicall Musicke*, London, 1597, modern edition R. A. Harman, London, 1952.

Since there has been a recent attempt by Fritz Rothschild to argue the opposite of what has just been said, and to suggest that crucial information with regard to tempo can and should be inferred from the time-signatures in conjunction with the value of the shortest notes found consistently in the piece itself, it may be as well to prove the point here by a reference to the contemporary authorities. It is true that Rothschild himself refers to a number of these authorities, but Thurston Dart, Walter Emery, and other experts are unanimous in considering that he has misunderstood them. (*See especially Walter Emery's review in Music and Letters, XXXIV, 3*).

But indeed no authority could make himself much plainer than the immensely learned and respected teacher (a man of weight in both the valuable and the tiresome senses of the word) Athanasius Kircher, who in 1650, after giving an unusually wide collection of C's stroked once (for twice as fast), stroked twice (for three times as fast), stroked three times (for four times as fast) and so, as he says, " ad infinitum," impatiently dismisses the entire series as " this most confused material " (hanc confusissimam materiam) and " utter rubbish " (tota farrago). Of the distinction to which Rothschild attaches most importance, that between C and ₵, Kircher merely remarks that he had found " the majority of the most distinguished musicians today " (i.e., remember, already prior to 1650), " and the most experienced in theory, to have omitted them, and to have everywhere taken them for one and the same sign " (pro unico signo). (*Athanasius Kircher, Musurgia Universalis, Rome*, 1650, *pp*. 679, 682 *and* 684).

Now Kircher was, if anything, a pedant; if there had been any sense to be got out of the old-fashioned time-signatures inherited by the baroque system from the Renaissance, Kircher would have been the man to get it. However, in case any reader of Rothschild still remains in doubt whether quite so much smoke could have been produced without a fire, here are a few other contemporary opinions.

" The signs . . . are superfluous and useless . . . everything is now in confusion." (*Pierre Maillant*, 1610).

" Measure, of which we ordinarily have but two kinds, duple and triple." (*de Caus*, 1615).

" Four-time which is marked "—interchangeably—" by a C or a

℄ stroked "; there is no way " of marking the degree of speed or slowness more precisely." (*Corette*, ? 1710).

" ℄, of which the usage is no longer well defined." (*Monteclair*, ? 1710).

" The movements " of common time " are very various." (*Malcolm*, 1731).

" Each interprets the character of the movement in the light of his own imagination." (*L'Abbé Laugier*, 1754).

J. S. Bach's use of time-signatures

In the light of the foregoing, we shall hardly expect to find Bach using his time-signatures accurately or consistently; nor do we. How, then, are we to interpret them in practice?

For the most part, this is not very difficult in the light of common sense and good musicianship, provided we remember well the first and only important rule: that choice of tempo comes not from the notation but from the implications of the music itself, as modified by the overall mood of the interpretation and the acoustic circumstances—in other words, by the peculiar conditions of the performance in question.

We may take first the two important common time signatures: C and ℄. Fundamentally, these are, in any baroque music including that of J. S. Bach, interchangeable. This is evidenced by passages in very numerous baroque authorities indeed, and is further made clear by the extremely casual use to which Bach puts them. He may even use C in one part and ℄ in another part of the same composition, where no practical difference exists or could have been intended whatsoever. However, while there is no fundamental difference, there is a certain tendency—we can put it no higher—for ℄ to hint at a faster time, perhaps only a very little faster, perhaps considerably faster, than C. Moreover (and this may be a little more definite and helpful in practice) there is a further tendency for ℄ to suggest a rhythm of two in a bar as opposed to the four in a bar most naturally associated with C.

Now we can easily realise that to hint at a faster time with no indication of how much faster does not take us very far, especially as the hint itself is only a tendency and not a reliable injunction. It may not so immediately be realised that the difference between two in a bar and four in a bar is almost as ambivalent. Yet we are constantly meeting with passages in which one conductor will beat two and another four, or which one performer will find it more natural to think of in two, and another in four. Except in fairly extreme cases, the musical effect to the ear may be very little different, if at all. In theory, of course, two in a bar means one accent in a bar, and four in a bar means two accents in a bar (the fact that on the organ accents are suggested by the articulation rather than directly effected does not alter the argument—the musical result is similar). In practice, this is exactly what happens in fairly extreme cases; but elsewhere, the question is a far more subtle one, since to mark every theoretical accent audibly is usually crude phrasing, to say the least of it. Bach's contemporary Geminiani specifically warned us that if " you lay a particular Stress on the Note at the Beginning of every Bar, so as to render it predominant over the rest, you alter and spoil the true Air of the Piece." (*Francesco Geminiani, The Art of Playing on the Violin, London,* ? 1741; *modern edition by David Boyden, New York,* 1953).

However, even in the most subtle phrasing the difference between a slight inclination to think in two or in four has some genuine bearing on the interpretation. The inclination towards two in a bar does tend to carry the music along rather more lightly than the inclination towards four in a bar. In many movements of J. S. Bach, particularly fugal movements, this added touch of lightness in the rhythm, this rather wider spacing of the accentuation and of the articulation which goes with the accentuation, can make all the difference between an earthbound and literally four-square performance on the one hand, and, on the other, a deliciously airborne and soaring performance, free from too much mechanical regularity.

Very often it will be found that in such cases J. S. Bach has in fact written ₵ rather than C; and especially when the length of his bar is the breve (four minims) as opposed to the semibreve (two minims). Indeed, once again in theory, a breve bar with ₵ (i.e. what is sometimes called Alla Breve time) equals a semibreve bar with C; and there are not infrequent occasions on which practice is so obliging as to correspond with theory. But we should be exceedingly naïve to expect this to be at all consistently the case.

$\frac{4}{4}$ or sometimes 4 was the commonly accepted equivalent of C, just as $\frac{2}{4}$ or 2 was of $\mathbb{C}$ (in breve time $\frac{8}{4}$ for C and $\frac{4}{2}$ for $\mathbb{C}$). That is why it was so revealing to find Bach's own statement that C is the same kind of time as 2. In short, both are duple time, and any difference of speed suggested by them, so far from being measured by a definite standard, is variable at will. The simplest answer to the puzzle, of course, is that there was no standard; only tendencies. Nothing could better illustrate the prevailing confusion between C and $\mathbb{C}$.

The use of 2 for $\mathbb{C}$ is especially French; the use of 3 for $\frac{3}{2}$ or $\frac{3}{4}$ is more general. Every baroque author seems a little (or a great deal) different in his account even of these apparently logical and straightforward signs based not on the half-circle stroked or reverted or otherwise, but on numbers. Movements in which the unit is a crotchet ($\frac{3}{4}$ or $\frac{6}{4}$ etc.) have certainly a disposition to move faster in terms of actual facts than those of which the unit is a minim ($\frac{3}{2}$ or $\frac{6}{2}$ etc.); those of which the unit is a quaver or a semiquaver ($\frac{3}{8}$, $\frac{6}{8}$, $\frac{3}{16}$, $\frac{6}{16}$ etc., etc.) faster again. But not even this simple rule is in the least to be counted on. The choice of unit often seems extraordinarily arbitrary, and there are plenty of movements with quaver unit which move slower than others with crotchet unit, and so on.

Thus although it would undoubtedly be an exaggeration to say that for purposes of tempo or even of rhythm the time-signatures in Bach's music can be ignored, the exaggeration would not be so gross a one as might at first be thought. Up to a point they not only can be ignored; they must be. That is to say, the decision as to the tempo of the music, and even as between a two-in-a-bar rhythm and a four-in-a-bar rhythm, has to be arrived at by the performer on his own initiative.

He must take this responsibility regardless of whether or not he has been able to glean some assistance from the time-signatures, and even, on occasion, in contradiction to what the time-signatures misleadingly assert. He must, admittedly, give them every consideration, and the more odd they seem the more he will consider them before dismissing them from his mind. But in the last resort he will need the courage and confidence to take his cue not from this or any other detail of the notation, but from what the music is telling him as a whole. It is never the notation which is decisive in baroque music—that music is far too casual and dependent on the performer's initiative for so simple a solution. It is always the implications of the music itself. Indeed, fundamentally this is always so; but it is even more so in baroque music than in subsequent music, for the reasons given in Chapter One above.

Time-signatures in Bach's organ music

(References are to the volume numbers of the Complete Bach Organ Works in Peters Edition.)

The Chorale Prelude, " Kyrie, Gott Vater in Ewigkeit," B.W.V. 669 (Vol. VII), is a normal example of breve time marked with ₵; count a moderate four in a bar. Compare the E major Fugue, No. IX, B.W.V. 878, from Book II of the Forty-Eight, which has the same notation, tempo (approximately) and rhythm. The effect intended by the stroke of the ₵ in cases such as this (which are as near " standard " as anything can be in this very flexible matter) is to make sure that the breve is thought of as a compound of four minims, not of eight crotchets. There is some baroque music in which the usual notation really is a breve bar of eight crotchet beats, sometimes—but only sometimes—reduced (by the implications of the music—the notation is no different) to four minim beats: e.g. the early seventeenth century English chamber music of the viols insofar as that is barred at all. Hence there is, or at least was once, some purpose in the stroke which ensures the four-beat version in this and the numerous parallel cases in J. S. Bach.

But then again, compare the E flat major Fugue, No. VII, B.W.V. 876, from Book II of the Forty-Eight, where the tempo and rhythm are in effect again very similar but not quite the same, the difference being shown with tolerable justification in the notation. The bar is a semi-breve, and the time-signature the stroked sign ₵; but this time the intention of the stroke could only be to suggest a two-in-a-bar rhythm. Now a rhythm of two minims in a semibreve bar and a rhythm of four minims in a breve bar are not very different; but they are just perceptibly so, since in the former there is the very slightest sense of a new beginning every two minims apart, and in the latter every four minims apart. This difference will undoubtedly be present in a sensitive interpretation; but whether it would not in any case be present, even if both fugues had been written in semibreve bars with ₵, or even with C or with no time-signature at all (when the theory is that C or $\frac{4}{4}$ is to be understood) is another question. Still, all these three instances are quite regular after their kind, and they are not without some logical consistency.

Other examples parallel to the Chorale Prelude just mentioned are: " Christe, aller Welt Trost," B.W.V. 670 (Vol. VII); " Kyrie, Gott heiliger Geist," B.W.V. 671 (Vol. VII); " Aus tiefer Noth," B.W.V. 686 (Vol. VI). The tempos, however, are not by any means all the same; and at least in the last named, the same effect could have been shown by writing crotchets in the place of minims and using common time of four crotchet beats to a bar. This is very commonly the case. However, it may be admitted that there is quite a good argument for many of these breve-bar ℂ alla breves, since this notation does undoubtedly suggest a broad four-beat sweep, and this breadth of rhythm is in keeping with the effect generally intended.

The G major Prelude and Fugue, B.W.V. 550 (Vol. IV), is marked in this generally reliable edition "Alla breve e staccato". Here the music implies a quick four in a bar and the notation seems inappropriate. The Chorale Prelude " Vater unser im Himmelreich," B.W.V. 737 (Vol. VII), has a breve bar with the very old-fashioned double-stroked ℂ; the intention, however, seems not illogical, since the implications of the music suggest counting two (i.e. two semibreves) not four in a bar, and moderately quickly at that.

The Chorale Prelude " Ich hab' mein' Sach' Gott heimgestellt," B.W.V. 707 (Vol. VI), is another " standard " semibreve bar with ℂ; count a moderately quick two in a bar. Contrast this, on the one hand, with the G major Fantasy for Organ, B.W.V. 572 (Vol. IV), a slow two-in-a-semibreve-bar (the following " lentement " has, indeed, a *slower* crotchet but sounds faster because of the demisemiquavers); and on the other hand with Duetto IV from the Clavieruebung, B.W.V. 805 (P.E. No. 4465), where a semibreve bar with the sign ℂ stands for a fairly quick four (not two) in a bar. In the third movement of the second Organ Sonata, B.W.V. 526 (Vol. I), there is an exceptional but quite intelligible use of the sign ₵, apparently equivalent to ℂ, and suggestive of a quick two in a bar —which suits the music.

There is no need to multiply examples of the use (and misuse) of C and ℂ. Sometimes these signs are used with logic and purpose, more often not, and provided the performer is relieved of the idea that he has to detect a purpose in them where none may exist, he will not find his responsibility particularly onerous.

The same may be said of the various triple-time signatures in the main. The Chorale Fugue "Allein Gott in der Hoeh' sei Ehr," B.W.V. 716 (Vol. VI), is in $\frac{3}{2}$, but the time is rather quick. The second movement of the first Organ Sonata, B.W.V. 525 (Vol. I), is an Adagio $\frac{12}{8}$; this wants a very steady four in a bar, yet is still rather quick for an adagio on the separate note-values (the speed is normal Siciliano in effect). Short notes more often move slower than one might expect, however, and long notes faster, in triple time. It is particularly important here to have no preconceived notions merely based on the visible appearance, and to let the effect of the music and not the notation govern the decision.

We next come to cases where the notation is not merely unhelpful or mildly misleading, but actually puzzling, at any rate at first sight. An extreme example is the Chorale Prelude, " Herr Gott, nun schleuss' den Himmel auf," B.W.V. 617 (Vol. V). There are three staves. The top bears the time-signature C; the middle, $C\frac{24}{16}$; the bottom, $C\frac{12}{8}$. The resolution, however, is surprisingly unsensational. The middle line has merely a " sextolet " relationship, and the bottom line a " triplet " relationship, to the top line. We have here, in short, an example of true proportional notation—but of that remnant of it which survived not merely into Bach's day, but into our own. It is merely the time-signatures which seem formidable; the effect is familiar enough. If Bach had omitted the two compound time-signatures and written C for all three parts, his intention would still have been clear, and no alarm caused. He could have made it still clearer by writing a small six against each group of sextolets and a small three against each group of triplets (as he has many times elsewhere); but even that would not have been necessary. However, we must admit that his actual method, if old-fashioned, was not less logical, and considerably more picturesque.

A rather simpler case of the same order occurs in the " 3 Versus " of "O Lamm Gottes, unschuldig," B.W.V. 656, as printed on p. 106 of the original Bach Gesellschaft Volume 25 (2). Up to this point all three staves have been in $\frac{3}{2}$; here, the top two staves go into $\frac{9}{4}$, the bottom remaining $\frac{3}{2}$ as before. The result is to put the crotchets of the top two parts into triplet relationship with the minim of the bass. In the Peters Edition (Vol. VII) this anomaly has been removed by giving the bottom stave also in $\frac{9}{4}$.

An amusing comparison may be found with Prelude XV, B.W.V. 860, from Book I of the Forty-Eight. Here Bach starts off with what are in effect ordinary semiquaver triplets in the treble stave. Against each of these triplets the bass has a single quaver. Instead, however, of either frankly admitting that the triplets are triplets, or alternatively putting the whole work, as he does so many others, equally frankly into compound triple time and dotting each of the quavers to make it the right length for its group of three semiquavers, Bach goes about it in the grand old-fashioned manner; he puts the treble stave into $\frac{24}{16}$ and the bass stave into C. So far, indeed, so tolerably good. We are quite prepared to humour him in the matter.

But no further on than bar three, a very natural complication arises. Bach wishes to reverse the roles: he does so; the quavers are now in the treble part, the groups of three semiquavers are now in the bass; the musical result is excellent. But what happens to the notation?

Nothing happens to the notation. The time-signatures remain as before, so that we now have genuine triplets (though not so marked) in the C of the bass; while in the $\frac{24}{16}$ of the treble we have what can only, in theory, be regarded as proportional quavers, the proportion being one quaver to the time value of three semiquavers. In practice, of course, nobody is going to worry what they are; the intention is transparently plain. The only factor which might conceivably put the player off is the compound time-signature (or rather the simultaneous use of two different time-signatures) being there at all. And if he has learnt anything about the essential nature of baroque notation, he will not let a little thing like that upset him. The essence of baroque notation is to put the intelligent performer on his mettle by trusting him with all the undefined details of its interpretation.

CHAPTER THREE

WORDS OF TEMPO

Time-words as vague as time-signatures

TIME-SIGNATURES, in spite of their name, do very little indeed towards establishing the tempo, and only a certain amount towards establishing the rhythm. There is, however, a system of verbal indication, or words of tempo, which first came into prominence in the course of the seventeenth century, after the proportional system of notation had substantially fallen obsolete.

The origin of these words of tempo is a most striking confirmation of the fact that what governs tempo is primarily the mood and character of the music itself; for the majority of them do not literally refer to speed at all, but to atmosphere. Adagio means " at ease "; Grave means " gravely "; Allegro means " cheerfully "; and so with many others. But it is their tempo meaning which prevailed, regardless of whether they are appropriate to the atmosphere or otherwise. There are many very tense adagios and melancholy allegros.

The attitude of Bach's contemporaries to the words of tempo as used by this master and others is as well summed up in the following passage as anywhere:

" Time is a various and undetermined thing . . . [There are] grave, adagio, largo, vivace, allegro, presto, and sometimes prestissimo. The first expresses the slowest Movement, and the rest gradually quicker; but indeed they leave it altogether to Practice to determine the precise Quantity . . . Movements of the same Name, as adagio or allegro, etc., are swifter in triple than in common time . . . the triple $\frac{3}{2}$ is ordinarily adagio, sometimes vivace; the $\frac{3}{4}$ is of any kind from adagio to allegro; the $\frac{3}{8}$ is allegro, or vivace; the $\frac{6}{4}, \frac{6}{8}, \frac{9}{8}$ are more frequently allegro; the $\frac{12}{8}$ is sometimes adagio but oftener allegro. Yet after all, the allegro of one species of triple is a quicker Movement than that of another, so very uncertain these Things are." (*Alexander Malcolm, A Treatise of Musick, Edinburgh*, 1731, *p.* 394).

This list of time-words in ascending order of speed is as typical as any, and is useful as a very general guide. But it cannot be emphasised too strongly that neither this nor any other such list, whether compiled in the baroque period or in modern times, can be depended upon as in any sense reliable. Thus, for example, Bach's contemporary and compatriot Quantz in 1752 treated largo as slower than adagio, and equated vivace with allegro. (*Joachim Quantz, Essay, Berlin*, 1752, *XVII*, 49). Brossard's Dictionary as pirated by Grassineau (1740) gives grave, adagio, largo; but the re-pirating by Hoyle (1770) gives adagio, grave, largo; while Cartier in 1798 comes up with largo, adagio, grave, and allegro, vivace. (*J. B. Cartier, L'Art du Violin, Paris*, 1798). And so on.

Quantz, in the passage cited, makes an attempt to give precision to the time-words by using as his reference the speed of the human pulse (itself variable, as he admits); he does so by arbitrarily gathering the many time-words into four groups to each of which he allots a tempo ranging from $\downarrow = 160$ for the fastest (which is very fast indeed) to $\downarrow = 40$ for the slowest. This is an interesting clue as to the outer extremes, but helps not at all in giving precision to the words themselves, since they were so obviously used by composers not in four neat groups but in a continuous gradation. Nor were other baroque attempts using the tick of a watch or the swing of a pendulum any more capable of solving the basic problem. It is not, in this sense of absolute measurement, soluble. There can only be relative solutions: i.e. relative to a given passage in a given performance.

Time-words in Bach's organ music

J. S. Bach uses rather few time-words in his organ music. They are not greatly missed; for even when they are present, as Quantz points out,

" . . . since many composers put these words more by habit than to characterise well the true movement of the pieces, and to assist the knowledge of their true time for those who render them, there are many cases where they cannot be used for guidance, and where it is necessary to divine the intention of the composer more from the content of the piece itself than from the word which is found at the head to indicate its movement." (*Joachim Quantz, Essay*, 1752, *XI*, 12).

Exactly so; the case could not be better put. Quantz warns us, however, against taking slow movements too slowly and fast ones too fast (*Ibid., XVII*, 7) ; adding that

" whatever speed an Allegro demands, it ought never to depart from a controlled and reasonable movement . . . The object must always be the passion which is to be expressed, never only to play fast." (*Ibid., XII*, 11).

This warning, and the opposite warning against " the error of a sluggish, dragging performance" (*C. P. E. Bach, Essay, Berlin*, 1753, *transl. Mitchell, London*, 1949, *p*. 152), occur so frequently in baroque authorities that we have certainly to take them seriously. Once more, however, they are in the most general terms; they are an appeal not to the performer's metronome, but to his musicianship.

CHAPTER FOUR

FLUCTUATIONS OF TEMPO

Fluctuations of tempo necessary in baroque music

THE right tempo for a given piece of music is not only a variable quantity, but a fluctuating one. I doubt if most musicians realise how flexibly their tempos fluctuate in course of the piece. They might be quite shocked to have it proved to them. Yet it is their instinctive flexibility which is right; it is their imagined strictness which would be wrong. As Bemetzrieder nicely put it in 1771: " taste is the true metronome". (*Leçons de Clavecin, Paris*, 1771).

This flexibility of tempo is just as appropriate to Bach's music as to any other. There is no general rule, of course. A series of very symmetrical sequences will always suggest a more regular tempo than, let us say, an expressive Sarabande. But a performer of Bach's organ music who believes that regularity of tempo is an obligation in music of this kind irrespective of the nature of the passage has been seriously misinformed. I am quite aware that a theory has been taught in some quarters to the effect that great reticence of feeling is needed to do true justice to baroque music. But this theory is not supported by any evidence from that period itself, and is in fact erroneous.

Among the long line of great organists whose teaching passed down in unbroken succession to J. S. Bach, we already find the Italian master Frescobaldi making perfectly plain in the early seventeenth century that in what was then modern music " the time is taken now slowly, now quickly, and even held in the air, according to the expression of the music "; while in particular the " cadences, though written rapid, should be played very sustained; and as you approach nearer to the close of the passage or cadence, you should hold up the time more and more" (*Girolamo Frescobaldi, Toccate, Rome*, 1614, *Preface*). Or as Mace put it in 1676, " sometimes Faster, and sometimes slower, as we perceive, the Nature of the Thing Requires " (*Thomas Mace, Musick's Monument, London*, 1676, *p.* 81). Jean Rousseau insisted that it is no use merely to "keep time . . . without entering into the movement " (*Jean Rousseau, Traité de la viole, Paris*, 1687, *p*. 81). And the good Quantz who so seldom fails us says that " the player must try to feel in himself not only the primary emotion," as suggested by " the word found at the beginning " (allegro, andante, adagio, etc.), " but all the others as they appear." He adds significantly that " in most pieces there is a perpetual alternation of emotions " (*Joachim Quantz, Essay, Berlin*, 1752, *XI*, 15).

It will be seen that all through the baroque period (and no doubt earlier), the ordinary flexibility of tempo which every good musician makes in following his natural feeling was accepted as part of normal expression. In practice, this flexibility is most evident at cadences. There is, of course, a considerable give and take at many points which are not cadences; but at cadences there is a more general need to mark a sense of rounding off, much as a reader may mark the closing of a paragraph. It is this need to which Frescobaldi drew attention in the quotation just given from the preface to his own organ Toccatas of 1614.

Not every cadence needs an actual ritardando. Indeed, there are so many cadences in the average piece of baroque music that to underline more than a small proportion of them in this way would make nonsense of the interpretation. But among these numerous cadences there will always be a few which the performer will feel, from the movement of the harmony, to be of greater weight and substance than the others. They represent a pause, more or less important, in the musical thought. It is these important cadences that need a ritardando of the kind described specifically by Frescobaldi.

We have here, I believe, one of the most crucial points in making a typical baroque piece of music sound properly at ease. To override the important cadences which punctuate the flow of the music from time to time is to give a curiously mechanical effect of remorselessness. This effect has been very common in the past, and is still more common than it ought to be; and it gives baroque music an undeservedly bad name for unfeelingness. It is not the only such misconception, since the mistaken idea of baroque music as orderly rather than emotional has affected every aspect of interpretation, but it is one of the most conspicuous. This is not, of course, a question of giving Bach a romanticised nineteenth-century interpretation of the very different kind which is right for Wagner or Elgar; that is the opposite extreme. It is a question of responding sensitively to the equally profound feeling which lies behind the orderly restraint of the great baroque composers. After all, in his own different manner Bach too is a romantic composer, as his harmony proclaims.

The notion that the tempo in Bach's music needs holding on a tight rein can be dismissed on the evidence of his own contemporaries as not only unnecessary, but out of character. Here, as elsewhere, it is only the implications of the music which can decide. It must, however, be added that in the great majority of cadences, however important, it will be enough to make a very slight ritardando. It must be perceptible, but not so much as to check the impetus of the movement. All that is required is to acknowledge the existence of the cadence; there is no need to rub it in. Yet this slight acknowledgement, in the momentary yielding of the tempo, of what is going on in the harmony, this mere hint of a ritardando in recognition of what the musical thought is undergoing, this modicum of tact and sensitivity will make all the difference between sewing-machine Bach and natural flexibility.

It was François Couperin, Bach's French contemporary and admired model, who spoke so feelingly of " the spirit, the soul that must be added " to the mere " quantity and equality of beats ". (*François Couperin, L'Art de toucher le Clavecin, Paris*, 1717, *p.* 38). Every good interpreter will recognise his meaning, and would be naturally inclined to give the music all the flexibility which such a phrase implies. But he may not always realise that he need have no inhibitions in doing so with Bach's music on the supposed grounds of authenticity. Actually, it is the over-disciplined performance which is unauthentic. Bach's own performances on the organ, which made so profound an impression at the time, were full of feeling.

Fluctuations of tempo in Bach's organ music

A definite change of tempo in the course of a movement will commonly, but not invariably, be shown by Bach with a new time-word at the appropriate point. Thus, for example, in bar 16 of the Preludium et Fuga for Organ No. II in D major, B.W.V. 532 (Vol.

IV), the words Alla breve denote a quicker time with a rhythmic feeling of two in a bar. The Fantasy and Fugue in A minor for Organ, B.W.V. 561 (Vol. IX), has at bar 12 the word Presto; at the end of bar 130 comes Adagio; four whole bars later (bar 135) there is an obvious return to the Presto, but this time-word itself is left out, presumably by accident. There is no real obscurity here, nor in other parallel cases; where doubt might arise Bach normally resolves it by the necessary instruction. The actual speeds themselves, of course, must be decided by intelligent musicianship in the usual way.

Ritardandos and other passing fluctuations of tempo are not as a rule indicated at all in baroque music, Bach's included. There is, however, one baroque practice which can cause misunderstanding if its intention has not been realised. This is the use of the ordinary time-words apparently to indicate a definite change of tempo at the point at which they appear, but actually to indicate something much more in the nature of a normal ritardando (we may compare the common use of *p* followed by *f* to mean a crescendo from the *p* to the *f*—not always so, of course—and of *f* followed by *p* to mean a diminuendo). The boundary is not always quite clear, but musical intelligence will usually decide the question without much difficulty in practice.

Thus the word Grave at the end of the Prelude of the Prelude and Fugue in G major for Organ, B.W.V. 550 (Vol. IV), and the word Adagio over the last bar of the B minor Organ Fugue, B.W.V. 579 (Vol. IV), have both of them, I think, the significance of a ritardando. They are typical of a great many similar instances throughout much baroque music—Corelli is particularly prone to them.

Now the final cadence of a movement is by definition the most important of any; hence no baroque performer, and no informed modern performer, would dream of arriving at it without a more or less conspicuous ritardando. Doubtless there are exceptions, but they are extremely rare and in the nature of special effects. The normal procedure is to slow down as soon as the cadential harmony begins strongly to demand it—not too soon, of course, but also not with that sudden jamming on of the brakes at the last possible moment which disfigures some performances.

Since this would be standard practice, what is the added meaning of the time-word? There are two possibilities: it may be there merely to make sure; or it may hint at what we should call " molto rit." The performer's judgment will easily decide. There is also the possibility that instead of a ritardando (or perhaps in addition to one) the time-word means literally what it says: namely what we should call " poco meno mosso." Once again, the music will give its own information provided that the performer is aware of the possibilities.

The last section of the organ C minor Fugue, B.W.V. 575 (Vol. IV), is headed " Piu lento," and yet the word Adagio appears over the last half-bar, with the fairly obvious meaning of ritardando. The word Grave ten bars from the end of the Adagio of the Toccata in C major for Organ, B.W.V. 564 (Vol. III), strikes me as equivalent to " poco meno mosso." We may compare Prelude 10 of the Forty-Eight, Bk. I, B.W.V. 855, where at bar 23 the word Presto is more a hint to unbutton than a sharp change of tempo. So too the word Presto at bar 28 of Prelude 2 of the Forty-Eight, Bk. I, B.W.V. 847. The Adagio at bar 34 of this Prelude is like a " poco meno mosso," and the Allegro at bar 35 like an " a tempo ". All such indications need intrepreting liberally and intelligently, however: and that is just as true of Beethoven's sudden Adagios or Prestos in the middle of his movements as it is of Bach's. It is in the nature of all true interpretation to be not literal but flexible and sensitive.

The Chorale Prelude " O Mensch, bewein' dein' Sunde gross," B.W.V. 622 (Vol. V), has Adagio assai followed by Adagissimo. I think we may take the hint and end this piece as if the close were " poco a poco ritardando." The Little Prelude and Fugue in E minor, B.W.V. 555, from the set of eight for organ, has at the end of the $\frac{3}{4}$ fugue two bars in $\frac{3}{2}$. Here we may feel that ♩ = ♩ and the effect is that of a written out ritardando to which little need be added. In other words, this is an effect not unlike a " poco meno mosso " ending, but more definite. And it will be appreciated that all the effects here described merge into one another; there are no hard and fast lines of division. Provided the performer remembers that nothing is literal and everything is flexible (and that this is still more true of baroque than of later notation) his own musicianship will do the rest.

CHAPTER FIVE

CONVENTIONS OF RHYTHM

The dot a variable quantity

THE dot placed after a note had more meanings than one in proportional notation. By the baroque period, it was confined to one meaning, and that basically the one which it has for us today. But whereas today we treat the dot fairly strictly as a symbol lengthening the time of the note before it by one half of its original value, the baroque musicians treated it as lengthening the time of the note before it by an indeterminate amount conditioned both by taste and circumstances.

It is true that we are not quite so strict today in practice as we like to think ourselves in theory. In any music, for example, with a march-like character to it, we tend to lengthen the dotted note quite considerably, shortening the note after it to correspond. Moreover, we tend to turn at least part of the value of this lengthened dot into a silence of articulation, thus crispening the texture at the same time as the rhythm. Nor are we entirely literal in our rendering of the dot in a number of other contexts. All this is very much in the spirit of baroque interpretation. The chief difference is that we take these liberties much less extensively, and without much awareness of doing so. The baroque musicians were very well aware of having a flexible convention for the treatment of dotted notes. They, too, would have described the dot as basically a means of lengthening a note-value by one half; but they were well aware of using this basis merely as a starting-point for any other length which might be convenient.

An important distinction has to be drawn here between (1) dotted notes which are an integral part of a true melodic line, on the one hand, and (2) dotted notes which comprise a rhythmic figure, on the other hand.

38

(1) Any true melodic line may contain a number of dotted notes scattered among others which are not dotted. In such cases there is often a possibility that the performer may very slightly prolong the dot and shorten the note after the dot, in the ordinary way of expression. But there is no convention, and was none in the baroque period, by which we may assume such treatment to be tacitly intended by the composer. If it is given at all, it is given as ordinary rubato, and the probability of it is scarcely if at all greater in baroque than in any other music.

(2) But if this melodic line consists, or largely consists, of a succession of dotted notes, or again if dotted notes occur not melodically in the true sense, but as an obvious rhythmic figure, then in baroque music there is not merely a possibility but a probability that the dot needs to be prolonged and the note after the dot shortened. This is not just ordinary expression such as might come with equal naturalness to a modern performer; it is a convention of interpretation, accepted as such by the baroque musicians, but now no longer current. It is part of the intentions of the composer, implied though not written in the notation, and to ignore it is as much a mistake as any other failure to read the notation correctly.

The evidence for this convention is widespread throughout the baroque literature of music, and there can be no possible doubt that it applies to the music of J. S. Bach. The contemporary explanations vary a little, as is natural with a convention whose precise application was deliberately left to the taste of the performer. But in the cases which come under this convention at all, the basis is that the dot itself becomes half as long again as it is written: or in other words, a dotted note is taken as if it were double-dotted.* Thus ♩. ♪ becomes in effect ♩.. ♪ and so forth.

Furthermore, the value certainly of the second dot and possibly of both dots is to be taken not as sound but as silence of articulation. Quantz explains that "the dotted note must be emphasized and the bow stopped during the dot" (*Joachim Quantz, Essay, Berlin*, 1752, *XI*, 13).

This gives ♩. ♪♪ or ♩ ♪ ♪♪ and so forth.

---

* The clearest and fullest explanation (too elaborate to quote here) is by Joachim Quantz, *Essay*, Berlin, 1752, V, 21 (p. 59 in Fr. Ed.).

But this basis itself can only be regarded as the starting-point. C. P. E. Bach assures us that " the short notes which follow dots are always made shorter than the written text indicates" (*C. P. E. Bach, Essay, Berlin*, 1753, *p.* 113). But he does not say how much shorter; and Quantz, whose illustrations are as given here, adds that he intends them only as approximate: " it is not possible to determine exactly the time of the little note which follows the dot " (*Joachim Quantz, Essay, Berlin*, 1752, *XI*, 21).

It is particularly to be observed that the frequent baroque cadential formula whereby the dominant chord carries a dotted note, followed by a shorter note which anticipates the tonic, comes under this convention. There is normally a further implication that the dotted note should carry a cadential trill. If the dotted note is taken trill-less and at literal value, the note of anticipation having its full written length, the effect is as ponderous and sluggish as a wet Sunday afternoon. It is still usual in modern performances, of course; but it is part of the misinterpretation from which baroque music has so long had to suffer. With the dotted note prolonged and trilled, and the note of anticipation delayed and shortened so that it is slipped in at the last possible moment before the tonic chord arrives, the effect becomes as gracious as its modern misinterpretation is clumsy.

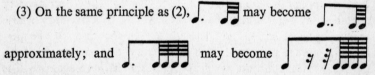

(3) On the same principle as (2),   may become   approximately; and   may become

approximately (the degree of articulation varies), and so forth. But in these cases the exceptions are much more numerous. We need to be particularly sure that a rhythmic figure rather than part of a true melodic outline is involved. Genuine cases do occur in Bach, but not very frequently. It is in French music, particularly in the typical French overture style, that this aspect of the convention is most in evidence—indeed, indispensable. The performer of Bach's organ music should be aware of its existence, but he will not often have to apply it, and if he fails to, the damage will not be serious, whereas if he fails to apply the aspect given under (2), he will emasculate many splendid passages of music.

(4) According to Quantz (*loc. cit.*) 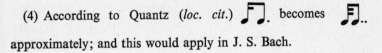 becomes

approximately; and this would apply in J. S. Bach.

(5) And ♪♪♪. becomes ♪♪♪.. approximately.

(6) It is particularly worth noting that ♩. ♪♪♪ and

♩. ♪♪♪ are neither of them meant to be a literal dotted

note followed by a triplet; they are both of them loose (but to a
baroque performer perfectly clear) ways of writing what is intended

to sound approximately ♩ ♪ ♪♪♪ (the degree of articula-

tion varies). Where we find ♩ ♪ ♪♪♪ in the notation, the

same interpretation (and not the literal one) is again often intended, though only if the circumstances enable us to take it as
a rhythmic figure of a kind requiring this increase of crispness.
In the majority of cases it will be obvious that the literal interpretation is the correct one here.

The French lilt

Early writers from Caccini in 1601, to Türk in 1789, give plentiful
illustrations of a species of expressive modifications of the written
rhythm to which many of them apply the general name of tempo
rubato—but in a special sense of this term rather different from
what it now conveys to us. We mean by it any expressive drawing
out of the tempo, whether restored by subsequent drawing in
(" borrowed time ") or never restored (" stolen time "). They
meant a redistribution of note-values within the bar, but without
disturbance to the total length of that bar. And they meant it in a
rather more definite sense than Chopin, for example, meant when he
asked for rubato in the right-hand melody but not in the left-hand
bass. They often meant what we should describe as a deliberate
syncopation, within the bar, of a melody written unsyncopated.

The last-mentioned effect can be ignored in Bach's music, not because it does not occur—it is of frequent occurrence—but because when it occurs it is written out more or less literally as it is intended to be performed. Places might be found where it could legitimately be added although not so written; but they would be rare and unimportant; and I have not noticed any in the organ works.

There are, however, other effects within this baroque category of tempo rubato (in their sense) which cannot so lightly be ignored. I have in mind, in particular, three which though probably French in origin and certainly more important in France than elsewhere, have nevertheless to some extent a European bearing. They were undoubtedly current in Germany, like much else that was of French provenance, during the period of J. S. Bach. In the case of Bach's harpsichord music, we have to remember that his style was largely founded on French models, and especially on Couperin. In the case of his organ music (with the possible and partial exception of the Organ Sonatas and, of course, his concerto transcriptions, as well as in their different way the Toccatas), his style was almost pure indigenous German, and the predominantly French conventions here in question are not often operative. But occasionally they are, and I think it is worth an organist's while to include a knowledge of them in his resources.

The general French name for this kind of rhythmic convention is " notes inégales." The three I have here in mind are commonly though not consistently called (1) the *lourer*; (2) the *couler*; (3) the *pointer*. (*See Quantz, loc. cit., for a full account*).

(1) The effect of the *lourer* is to give a swinging lilt to a series of notes, neither very fast nor very slow, of which the notation is even but the performance is made somewhat uneven, " because," said Saint-Lambert in 1702, " this unevenness makes them more graceful " (*Saint-Lambert, Principes du clavecin, Paris*, 1702). The effect was only introduced in movements of a serene or tender character, not in those of forceful or virile character; above all in Sarabandes; only very doubtfully (most authorities disfavoured it) in Allemandes; never, I should say, in a March or a Bourrée. The notes affected are, normally, the shortest to appear with any frequency in the movement concerned. They may go four to a beat or two to a beat—never three and never one. They must not be either too fast

or too slow to be gracefully treated in this way: quavers or semi-quavers are the commonest. They must be mainly conjunct and melodic; they must fall easily into pairs. If they are written slurred in pairs, the hint to make them unequal is very strong indeed; if they are written slurred by fours, or any other number greater than two, this kind of inequality is wholly ruled out. It may also be ruled out by written directions: " notes égales "; " marquées "; " martelées"; " detachez"; "mouvement décidé "; etc.—or by dots or dashes under or above the notes.

The inequality is not definitely measured, but may usually give the first of each pair about twice as long as the second. The effect to the ear is more or less that of triplet rhythm—or to put the same thing in another way, of turning e.g. common time into compound-triple time.

(2) Under similar circumstances, the *couler* may be applied instead. So far from giving a lilt to the music, this makes it rather jerky and agitated: the first of each pair is shortened to about a quarter and the second lengthened to about three quarters of the total value—or the proportions may be yet more exaggerated. This amounts to more or less of a Scotch snap. It is occasionally indicated by slurring each pair but with a dot below or above the second note; it may be used where not indicated, but with discretion, and far less frequently than the *lourer*. Spitta quotes a case from the Credo of Bach's B Minor Mass where this effect is written out at first, but left to the performer to carry on subsequently. (*Spitta, J. S. Bach, Leipzig*, 1873-80, *transl. C. Bell and J. A. Fuller-Maitland, London*, 1884-85, *III*, 49). It is admissible in the organ works, but far from indispensable.

(3) The *pointer* simply means that written dotted notes which turn up among notes written evenly but performed unevenly as *lourer* or *couler* need performing more unevenly than they are written. This is merely a special instance of what has been described in the preceding section as to the baroque treatment of dotted notes in general.

Casual inaccuracies in the notation of rhythm

We have already mentioned that the dot may be used elastically to prolong the note before it to any convenient extent. This may be done, as we have seen, for directly expressive purposes, to crispen up the rhythm; it may also be done merely to save a careful but

troublesome use of ties: ♩. ♫♫ is easier to write than

♩ ♫♫♫ and the baroque performer could be trusted to

take the meaning without difficulty. He would in any case tend to extend the value of the main note, and to delay and shorten the little notes after it, whatever the notation. Nor would it confuse him if more or fewer little notes appear than the mathematical feasible quota; he would in any case take them all in a bunch at the last possible moment. The French composers were particularly apt to flout the merely mathematical possibilities in this way. J. S. Bach was particularly careful not to; but this care was not invariable; nor did it extend to other aspects of his notation of rhythm. In those which follow we have to know the contemporary conventions if we are to read his notation correctly, since it is decidedly misleading as it is written.

These are the conventions which allowed what are in effect compound triple rhythms to be written inaccurately as simple (or sometimes as a mixture of the two). Here, too, we can see the lingering remnants of the old proportional system of notation, though not here very logically applied. "Although the values of the treble do not seem to fit with those of the Bass," writes Couperin at one point in his own harpsichord music, " it is customary to write thus ". (*François Couperin, Pièces de Clavecin, Book Two, Paris,* 1717, 10*th Ordre, note*).

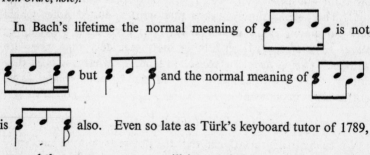

In Bach's lifetime the normal meaning of ⸬. ♪♪ ⸬ is not

⸬♪♪⸬ but ⸬♪ ⸬ and the normal meaning of ⸬ ♪♪ ⸬

is ⸬♪ ⸬ also. Even so late as Türk's keyboard tutor of 1789,

we read that some composers still intended this conventional usage, although others (Mozart among them) intended not the conventional but the literal interpretation. (*Clavierschule, Leipzig and Halle,* 1789). In J. S. Bach the literal interpretation is nearly always merely an incorrect interpretation, though doubt arises in some examples, as we shall see below.

Conventions of rhythm in Bach's organ music

We must start by realising that Bach was perfectly capable of writing out the most elaborate simple-plus-compound triple, dotted and double dotted rhythms with complete precision, using all the necessary triplets and ties (the double-dot itself though known earlier only came into fashion a generation later) when he so chose. An excellent example to prove this point is Prelude XIV, B.W.V. 883, from Book Two of the Forty-Eight. But he did not always so choose.

A clear case for " double-dotting " in the sharpest French style, with the sound of the dots replaced by silences of articulation, will be found in the E flat Prelude for Organ, B.W.V. 552 (Vol. III), from Clavieruebung, Dritter Theil. We may compare Fugue V, B.W.V. 850, from Book I of the Forty-Eight, where the style is highly French and crisp, with the dotted quavers of the subject simply crying out to be " double-dotted " throughout.

An equally clear case for *not* " double-dotting " can be seen in bars 15, 27, 29-32, etc., of the Chorale Fantasia for Organ, " Valet will ich dir geben," B.W.V. 735 (Vol. VII). The reason is that the rhythm is not open and unconstrained; there are other moving parts to be fitted within the time of the dots themselves. Wherever this kind of rhythmic dovetailing occurs we are normally precluded from introducing any expressive irregularity into the rhythm (there may be exceptions, but if so they would certainly be special cases). Dovetailing occurs again in the Chorale Variation VII on " Christ, der du bist der helle Tag," B.W.V. 766 (Vol. V), and, of course, countless other passages in baroque music.

It must be understood that the conventions for " double-dotting " apply to rests as much as to notes. Thus in the G major Prelude for organ, B.W.V. 568 (Vol. VIII), we should " double-dot " (with marked silences of articulation), starting in bar 8, but perhaps excepting bars 45-46. Ex. 1 shows bar 13 as written, and Ex. 2 as conventionally performed.

Now for some mixed or doubtful or complicated cases. In the organ Toccata No. I in C major, B.W.V. 564 (Vol. III), we meet with several characteristic problems. In bar 24 the dotted quaver B is to be prolonged and trilled, the semi-quaver following being delayed and shortened. In bar 27 the last beat has a dotted note which is not a rhythmic figure but an integral part of the melody; it should be played as written. But in bars 30-31 the dotted notes make, on the contrary, rhythmic figures; they need sharpening by some degree of " double-dotting " and some crispness of articulation. In bar 31 the rest before the last semiquaver chord needs to be lengthened, and this semiquaver chord itself needs to be taken at demi-semiquaver value. So too the first beat of bar 32. But bar 33 has semiquavers moving within the time of the dots and I suggest an exactly literal rhythm.

If that is to be done, of course, it is quite possible to argue from this that all the dotting in this piece should be taken literally to preserve the logic. But logic has only a certain modified validity in a matter such as this, and the rendering I have suggested is the one which I am fairly certain would have occurred most naturally to the great majority of performers in Bach's own day, and was probably more or less what Bach would himself have done. It must be remembered that there is never any one right way in musical interpretation, with all the others wrong, and least of all so in baroque music where so much more was left in the hands of the performer than we are accustomed to leave. His taste was the arbiter; but baroque taste ran strongly in the direction of sharpened rhythms and crispened articulation, and if we want to make the most of its characteristic brilliance, we shall follow suit.

In the same Toccata, the C Adagio which follows needs to have its dotted notes sharpened and crispened to a very marked degree. Altogether, it should be remembered, Toccata style is brilliant, flamboyant, improvisatory, with a distinct relationship to the brilliance of French overture style; and to this effect the brilliance of the sharpened rhythm very greatly contributes.

I have mentioned, in the last paragraph but one, an instance of the connection between ornamentation and rhythm; a few further examples of this connection may be helpful. In the first movement of the second Organ Sonata, B.W.V. 526 (Vol. I), the Vivace (a ₡ with quick four in a bar) at bar 16 a cadential formula occurs which strongly suggests, though without actually enforcing, a conventional ornamentation further necessitating a modification of rhythm (the trills, by the way, are indispensable—it is only the turns which are optional). Ex. 3 shows bar 16 as written, and as conventionally performed.

Three typical and instructive examples may be given from the third movement (allegro) of the same work, in bars 29, 40, and 57. The movement contains many others and so do most movements by J. S. Bach. So far as rhythm is concerned, however, the principles are the same although the details vary; and so far as ornamentation is concerned, its many problems will be found discussed in a companion volume in the present series, and will not be further touched upon here.

Ex. 4, 5 and 6 show bars 29, 40 and 57 as written, and as conventionally performed.

Both in bar 29 and in bar 57, the first dotted note might be double-dotted if desired, but I should not myself do this. The ornaments, however, with the rhythmic alterations which go with them, are indispensable, whether indicated by signs (as they are here except for the top line in bar 57) or not. For signs of ornamentation in most baroque music, including Bach's, are the most casual of hints (the chief exceptions are Couperin and others of the French school—whom in this respect, unfortunately, Bach did *not* emulate). Like the rhythmic matters with which they are so closely bound up, they were governed not by the notation but by the understood conventions and the trained imagination of the performer.

The French lilt or *lourer* can often be applied with good historical justification and excellent musical effect in Bach's harpsichord music, since so much of it is under French influence; in his organ music very seldom, but I think the Chorale Prelude " O Lamm Gottes, unschuldig," B.W.V. 618 (Vol. V), with its original slurs over pairs of semiquavers, is a genuine case for it: Ex. 7 shows it as written, and with *lourer*.

The *lourer* introduces rhythmic unevenness (approximately as a triplet) where none is written. Of the opposite effect of reducing the written inequality of a dotted note to triplet proportions, a good example is in bars 17, 21 and 38 of Bach's organ transcriptions of Vivaldi concertos, No. 1 in G major, B.W.V. 592 (Vol. VIII), first movement. Here the 𝅘𝅥𝅭 𝅘𝅥𝅮 becomes 𝅘𝅥 𝅘𝅥𝅮 (3) in performance.

But not so in bar 44 where, on the contrary, both the dotted notes carry ornaments and should be " double-dotted," as also in bar 53. Yet in bars 58-63, we should again reduce the dots to triplet rhythm, fitting them to the prevailing 3-quaver movement, not contrasting them with it. Nor are we yet at the end of our difficulties; for in bar 71 we find a dotted rhythm set against four even semiquavers, and here we should take the dot exactly as it is written in order to preserve a perfect fit. We have again to " double-dot " with ornaments, in bar 72; to take exactly as written, on account of the dovetailing, the first dotted note in bar 91, while " double-dotting," with ornament, the second; and so forth in the rest of this very taxing movement. Not that my advice is necessarily the best in any given instance; but that is the kind of treatment the evidence shows a contemporary performer would have meted out. The modern performer, like the contemporary performer, will very properly reach his own conclusions in detail. But in general, these will be wrong if they ignore the conventions entirely and trust to a literal rendering which was demonstrably alien to Bach's own intentions.

The second movement (grave) of the same concerto requires thorough-going " double-dotting " of a consistent nature, and thus not difficult to establish. The last movement (allegro) of the second concerto, in A minor, B.W.V. 593 (Vol. VIII), in bar 59, etc., needs the up-beat semiquaver chords to be delayed by a further demi-semiquaver rest, and then taken at demi-semiquaver value. Some unevenness, not really amounting to " double-dotting," may be suggested for the " Recitative, Adagio " in the second movement of the third concerto, in C major, B.W.V. 594 (Vol. VIII).

In the Chorale Prelude, " Kommst du nun, Jesu, vom Himmel herunter," B.W.V. 650 (Vol. VII), of which the time-signature is $\frac{9}{8}$, we find in bars 26, 38 and 42, dotted quavers with semiquavers set against three equal quavers. The dotted rhythm should be reduced to "triplet" rhythm, with the dotted quavers made into crotchets and their semiquavers made into quavers. (See the beginning of the previous paragraph but one).

In the Chorale Prelude "In dulci jubilo," B.W.V. 608 (Vol. V), matters are not so straightforward. The time-signature is $\frac{3}{2}$, and we find:

Ex. 8   bar 3   bar 11   bar 25

It can be argued that since Bach wrote triplet crotchet plus quaver in bar 25 (alto part) he did *not* want that same effect introduced in bar 3, bar 11, etc., where he did not write it. If that is correct, bars 3 and 11, etc., should be performed, as written, with a "two-against-three" effect.

But equally it can be argued that Bach's notation (sharing as it did in the calculated impreciseness of nearly all notation of that period) cannot be relied upon to mean what it says even in such a case as this; and indeed the inconsistency of writing the same effect one way in bar 3 or bar 11 and another way in bar 25 would be no greater than many other inconsistencies which we can prove elsewhere in Bach's notation. If this second argument is correct, we should take the crotchets in bars 3 and 11, etc., unevenly to match the triplet rhythm as established (in writing) by the tenor part of bar 3. In other words, we should take the untied crotchets in bars 3 and 11 as if they were written (apart from the ties) exactly as they are in fact written in bar 25, alto part.

I believe this second hypothesis is the more probable, but the case is exceptionally doubtful, and I should certainly not be prepared to dismiss either alternative. One contemporary performer might have preferred the first solution, another the second—and both would have been right in the sense of being well within the possible meanings of the notation and, I think, the implications of the music.

One final case of doubt and complexity may be given, from the third movement of the fourth Organ Sonata, B.W.V. 528 (Vol. I), this movement being headed " Un poco Allegro " with the time-signature $\frac{3}{8}$. As the title suggests, the tempo is not so fast as the mere three quavers to a bar might at first suggest, and it is definitely a case for three in a bar, not one in a bar. The main rhythm is triplet semiquavers against quavers in the bass, one quaver to a beat. In bar 7, however, we have semiquavers two to a quaver, not three. I am almost sure that a contemporary performer coming on this in the context of so many written triplets already established would have played these evenly written semiquavers also triplet fashion, i.e., unevenly. Ex. 9 shows bar 7 as written, and as conventionally performed.

This seems to be conclusively confirmed in bar 15, where the evenly-written semiquavers and the written-out triplet semiquavers come together. In the light of the overall picture presented by the contemporary baroque evidence, I find it almost impossible to believe that Bach's intentions were anything but the following. Ex. 10 shows bar 15 as written, and as conventionally performed.

This is what a contemporary performer, or at any rate what most contemporary performers, would have done, without a second thought, on reading the piece through. But in bar 25, he would have come on a passage which might well have given him second thoughts, and certainly does me. For now we find set against the semiquaver triplets not evenly written semiquavers but semiquavers written dotted with demi-semiquavers after them. Nothing could be more natural for a baroque performer than to reduce them to the same triplet rhythm to which the previous evenly written semi-quavers have already been extended—except that, if so, we have once again two different ways of writing the same effect within a few bars of each other in the same piece of music. Shall we then dismiss this (as I was, though not without hesitation, inclined to do with the previous example from " In dulci jubilo ") as yet one more characteristically baroque inconsistency of notation? In this par-ticular case, I have still less hesitation in doing just that, because of what is written in bars 90-91, as Ex. 11 shows.

In the previous example from " In dulci jubilo," two views could be taken as to which rendering makes the best musical effect, the literal one or the conventional. In the present instance, I cannot feel that this question is open to any real doubt. Played literally as written, these two bars sound simply messy. The rhythm is exceedingly complex (especially on beat two of bar 90), tricky to bring off and unsatisfying to the ear; the passing discords both arrive and depart awkwardly (notice how the first E in the treble part would sound first against the D sharp and then against the F sharp in the middle part); the whole impression is unconvincing once the perfectly simple alternative is appreciated. This alternative, which it is virtually certain that Bach intended and that any competent contemporary performer of his would have arrived at, on third thoughts if not on first or second, is shown in Ex. 12.

In other words, for all its complexity in appearance, this case is not complex at all in its solution. I know of none more typical either of the laxness of notation in so much baroque music, or of the efficacy of the appropriate tacit convention in producing a practical solution once the performer is aware of it.

Does this system of trusting as much to the performer and as little to the notation as possible appear unreasonably difficult? It is far less so in practice than it seems on paper. It is, above all, addressed to the innate musicality of the performer, and that is a commodity which we still possess.

ANNOTATED BOOK LIST

for further reading

Bach Section. Hinrichsen's Seventh Music Book, pp. 263-444. London, 1952. A treasury of detailed information and discussion.

Bach, C. P. E. *Essay on the True Art of Playing Keyboard Instruments.* Berlin, 1753-1762, tr. W. J. Mitchell, London, 1949. One of the most important and influential treatises on music ever written, and invaluable for a general understanding of J. S. Bach's performing style (but some allowances must be made for changes between the two generations).

Dart, Thurston. *The Interpretation of Music.* London, 1954. The entire approach is exactly what the subject requires, and an astonishing amount of accurate and helpful information and suggestion is included within a comparatively narrow space. Excellent both on tempo and on rhythm of the period of J. S. Bach.

Dolmetsch, Arnold. *The Interpretation of the Music of the 17th and 18th Centuries.* London (1914). Still the most reliable and informative introduction to the subject. Its author's individuality comes through so clearly and valuably that the book will never be altogether superseded. Gives much detailed help on tempo and rhythm.

Donington, Robert. *Baroque Interpretation.* *Grove's Dictionary of Music and Musicians.* London, 5th Ed., 1954, Vol. I, p. 444, and kindred articles there referred to.

[**Donington, Robert.** *Tempo and Rhythm in Bach's Organ Music.* London, 1960].

Donington, Robert. *The Interpretation of Early Music.* London (1961). An overall survey in extensive detail, including a lengthy discussion of tempo and rhythm.

Mozart, Leopold. *Treatise on the Fundamental Principles of Violin Playing.* Augsburg, 1756, tr. E. Knocker, London, 1948. Besides being necessary to violinists, this valuable treatise is helpful to a general understanding of J. S. Bach's performing style.

Rothschild, Fritz. *The Lost Tradition in Music.* London, 1953. Solely concerned with tempo and rhythm in J. S. Bach and his period: unfortunately an almost totally mistaken though sincere book (See reference on p. 22).

Sachs, Curt. *Rhythm and Tempo.* New York, 1953. Probably the most important modern study of the subject over the entire historical range. Includes a detailed examination of proportional notation and its remnants in the period of J. S. Bach. Not an infallible book (what book is?), but sane, informative and illuminating, with an unusually wide field of vision.

Sumner, William L. *The Organ of Bach.* Hinrichsen's Eighth Music Book. London, 1956. Contains what is in effect a short book on the Organ of Bach, and a large number of articles relating to Bach's organ music by other authorities of equal excellence. A most necessary study for Bach organists.

COMBINED PERSONAL AND SUBJECTIVAL INDEX

C. P. E. Bach, J. S. Bach, Beethoven, Bemetzrieder, Brossard, Caccini, Cartier, de Caus, Chopin, Corelli, Couperin, Dart, Elgar, Emery, Frescobaldi, Galilei, Geminiani, Hoyle, Kircher, Langier, Mace, Maelzel, Maillant, Malcolm, Montéclair, Morley, Mozart, Quantz, Rothschild, Rousseau, Saint-Lambert, Spitta, Türk, Vivaldi, Wagner

SCHOOL OF BACH-PLAYING FOR THE ORGANIST

A series of guide books and music
covering various aspects of organ-playing
as applicable to the works of
J. S. Bach

General Editor: Gordon Phillips

ARTICULATION
IN ORGAN PLAYING*

A " Little Organ Book " for Manuals only
based on 31 Chorale Preludes and Chorales by Bach
arranged in the order of the Liturgical Year

by Gordon Phillips

With a Foreword by Robert Donington

BACH'S ORGAN REGISTRATION†
AND ALLIED MATTERS

by William L. Sumner

With a Foreword by Ivor Keys

TEMPO AND RHYTHM
IN BACH'S ORGAN MUSIC†

by Robert Donington

With a Foreword by Gordon Phillips

BACH'S ART OF PART-PLAYING*

by Stainton de B. Taylor

A collection of six short Trios

with advice on registration and method of study

BACH'S METHOD OF TRIO-PLAYING*

The 2-part Inventions, arranged as Trios, with a third part added

by Max Reger and Karl Straube

(Not for sale in the U.S.A. and Canada)

BACH'S ART OF FUGUE*

The complete work laid out for the organ in an eminently
practical manner.

by Hans Schuricht

FIGURED BASS BACH STUDIES*

Bach's 69 Sacred Songs and Arias from ' Schemelli's Musicalisches
Gesangbuch of 1736 ' are among the most beautiful religious music.
They offer the greatest possible inspiration to those who are working
on the realisation of figured bass. The melodies are printed in
the soprano clef and the basses left just as Bach wrote them. Most
suitable for practice besides the mechanical exercises offered in
text-books.

(further volumes in preparation)

*=music.   †=book.

BOOKS ON BACH AND BACH FACSIMILES

(b) in English :

Art (The) of J. S. Bach. A comprehensive study *by A. E. F. Dickinson*, with many musical and pictorial Illustrations, a Glossary, Bibliography, Index to the music discussed, and a Numerical List of the Choral Cantatas, also classified according to the Church Year. Second enlarged edition. No. S-13.

Articulation in Organ-Playing. A " Little Organ Book " for Manuals only, *by Gordon Phillips*. Based on 31 Chorale Preludes and Chorales by Bach, and arranged in the order of the Liturgical Year. With *Foreword by Robert Donington*. No. H-1001.

Bach Bicentenary Calendar, with Reproductions of Paintings and Drawings of Bach and his Family, with Facsimile Examples from their Compositions, several published for the first time. No. H-502.

Bach Biography (A short), *by Esther Meynell*. No. D-121.

Bach's Musical Structure. A 50-page study. Contained in " Challenge to Musical Tradition " *by A. T. Katz*. No. H-382.

Bach's Organ-Registration, *by William L. Sumner*. With *Foreword by Ivor Keys*. The German Organ in Bach's Time - The Nature of the Stops in the Organs played by Bach - The Use of the Divisions of the Organ - Pro Organo Pleno - Doppio Pedale - The young Bach's Expert Advice - Ein' feste Burg - Tremulant and The Cymbelstern - Phrasing and Touch - Some other accounts of Organ-registration in the 17th and early 18th Centuries. No. H-1002.

Brandenburg Concertos. The six. Facsimile Edition de luxe, with *Foreword by Ralph Kirkpatrick*. No. D-29.

Fantasia super ' Veni sancte spiritus ' (Come, Holy Ghost), in Facsimile, with Bach Portrait and Critical Analysis *by Peter Wackernagel*. No. D-117.

Inventions (two- and three-part), prefaced *by Ralph Kirkpatrick*. " The study of the Facsimile of this MS. is one of the greatest music lessons of a life-time." (*Musical America*). No. P-4201a.

Organ (The) of Bach and **Gottfried Silbermann, Organ Builder,** *by William L. Sumner*; **The Organ Music of Bach,** *by Albert Riemenscheider and Herman Keller*. Including also: A Grading System - The Tempo of Bach's Organ Works - Bach Organ Recital Syllabus - Bach's Clavier Music - The Nicknames of the Organ Fugues - 45 Organ Specifications incl. those of every Organ on which J. S. B. is said to have played. Contained in Hinrichsen's Eighth Music Book. No. H-1956.

BOOKS ON BACH

Samuel Wesley's Famous Bach Letters (1808-1816), and related matters, with Introduction *by Harold Helman.* Various Portraits and Facsimiles. Fourth (enlarged) edition. No. H-1958b.

Tempo and Rhythm in Bach's Organ Music, *by Robert Donington.* Tempo as a Performer's Responsibility - Time Signatures - Words of Tempo - Fluctuations of Tempo - Conventions of Rhythm. With *Foreword by Gordon Phillips.* No. H-1003.

Violoncello Solo Suites. Numbered edition, two parts in one cover, in the size of the original. Facsimile of the complete MS. together with an engraved (un-edited) edition. No. D-12.

(*a*) *in German :*

Bach Congress 1950 in Leipzig. With Contributions by numerous international Bach Scholars, among them *D. Bartha, H. Besseler, W. Blankenburg, S. Borris, M. Dehnert, H. H. Draeger, A. Duerr, H. H. Eggebrecht, E. Flade, W. Gurlitt, K. Laux, Jos. Marx, E. H. Meyer, F. Oberborbeck, W. Schmieder, E. Schmitz, W. Serauky, D. Shostakovich, H. Sievers, W. Vetter,* etc. No. D-675.

Bachs Leben, Kunst und Kunstwerke, *by J. N. Forkel,* with a Portrait and 18 Musical Examples. Facsimile print from the first edition (published in 1802 in the Peters Edition). No. De-112.

Bachs Weltliche Kantaten. A musicological survey of the secular Cantatas, *by Ian Finlay.* No. De-119.

Der Thomaskantor. A study with numerous Illustrations, *by A. Strube.* No. De-686.

Die Klavier-Werke Bachs. Ein Beitrag zu ihrer Geschichte, Form, Deutung und Wiedergabe, *by Hermann Keller,* with many musical Illustrations. No. P-4571.

Die Orgel-Werke Bachs. A contribution to the History, Form, Interpretation and Performance of Bach's Organ Works, *by Hermann Keller.* A book of reference for the performer and student of Bach's Organ Works. Many musical Illustrations. No. P-4572.

Goethe's Relationship to Bach, *by Friedrich Smend.* No. D-680.

THE COMPLETE ORGAN WORKS OF BACH

in nine Volumes

Hermann Keller, in 'The Organ Works of Bach,' gives credit to the authoritative Griepenkerl-Peters Edition of the Bach Organ Works as the first in value. He assigns the Bach Gesellschaft edition second place, since numerous important Manuscript copies, which were available to Griepenkerl, were lost soon afterwards.

1. Passacaglia & Fugue C m.; Pastorale F; 6 Trio Sonatas. (P-240)

2. Fantasia & Fugue G m. (*Great*); 9 Preludes & Fugues: C (*Weimar*), G (*Great*), A. F m., C m. (*Great*), C (*Leipzig*), A m. (*Great*), E m. (*Wedge* or *Scissors*), B m. (*Great*). (P-241)

3. Fantasia & Fugue C m.; 6 Preludes & Fugues: E flat (*St. Anne's* or *Trinity*), D m. (*Violin Fugue*), G m., C, A m., E m. (*Cathedral, Little, or Nightwatchman*); 3 Toc-catas and Fugues: F, D m. (*Dorian*), C. (P-242)

4. Canzona D m.; 2 Fantasias: G, C m.; 4 Fugues: C m. (*Legrenzi* or *Double Fugue*), G m. (*Little* or *Folksong*), B m. (*Corelli*), C m.; Praeludium A m.; 4 Preludes & Fugues: C (*Trumpet*), G, D, C m. (*Arnstadt*); Toccata & Fugue D m.; Trio D m. (P-243)

5. 56 Short Chorale Preludes; 5 Canonic Vars. on '*Vom Himmel hoch*'; 7 Chorale Preludes; Chorale Vars. on '*Christ, der du bist der helle Tag*,' on '*O Gott, du frommer Gott*,' on '*Sei gegruesset Jesu guetig*' (easy). (P-244)

6. 34 Chorale Preludes (Chorales A to J), incl. '*Schuebler*' No. 5; '*18 Great Chorales*' Nos. 3, 5, 12, 13 to 16; *Clavieruebung*, Part III Nos. 7 to 11, 16 to 21. (P-245)

7. Chorale Preludes (Chorales K to Z), incl. No. 60: '*Wir glauben all' an einen Gott*' (The Giant Fugue or The Credo); '*Schuebler*' Nos. 1 to 4, 6; '*18 Great Chorales*' Nos. 1, 2, 4, 6 to 11, 17, 18; *Clavieruebung* Part III Nos. 1 to 6, 12 to 15. (P-246)

8. Allabreve D; 4 Concerti: G, A m. (*Vivaldi*), C (*Vivaldi*), C; Fantasia C; 2 Fugues: C (*Hexachord*), G m.; 3 Preludes: C, C, G; 8 Short Preludes & Fugues: C, D m., E m., F, G, G m., A m., B flat. (P-247)

9. Aria F; 14 Chorale Preludes; Partita: Chorale Variations on '*Ach, was soll ich Suender machen*'; Fantasia G (5th Concerto); Fantasia con imitazione B m.; Fantasia and Fugue A m.; 2 Fugues: G (*Fugue à la Gigue*), G; A Short Harmonical Labyrinthus C m.; Pedal-Exercitium G m.; 3 Trios: G, G (*Telemann*), C m. (P-2067)

BACH'S ORGAN WORKS BASED ON CHORALES

in three Volumes

This new collection follows in every respect the liturgical sequence used by Bach himself and can be regarded as an authoritative edition

1. The Little Organ Book (*Orgelbüchlein*). 45 Chorale Preludes (P-3946)
2. The six Schuebler Chorales and the eighteen Chorales (P-3947)
3. Clavieruebung, Part III with Catechism Preludes and the four Duettos (P-3948)

OTHER BACH CHORALE PRELUDE COLLECTIONS

in five Volumes

1. Chorale Preludes *for Christmas* (P-2676d)
2. Chorale Preludes (thirty) *in progressive order* (P-2178b)
3. Chorale Preludes from Clavieruebung, *re-arranged for small hands*, manuals only (H-376)
   – from the above: Allein Gott; Aus tiefer Noth (H-376a)
4. Chorales extended, from 3 Church Cantatas: Nos. 4, 24, 129: Christ Jesus, only Son of God; O God, Thou God of Faith; Let Heaven and Earth rejoice (H-353)
5. Preludes (three) on '*In dulci jubilo*,' preceded by Bach's choral setting (H-356)

MISCELLANEOUS BACH ORGAN WORKS

(a) *on two staves:*

Album of Original Bach Works. This new collection of 24 pieces on two staves, edited by Hermann Keller, includes only compositions especially suitable for small organ. Entrata F; Menuet and Trio F; Bourrée A; Menuet Eb; Sarabande Bb; Praeludiums; C, G, D m ; Andante F; Adagio D m.; Vivaldi Organ Concerto A m.; Fugatos: E m., G; Fantasias: C, D m.; Fuga D m.; Andante C; Larghetto C m. and Vivace F *from the Pastorale*; Fuga D m. *from 'The Art of Fugue'*; Aria D; Fantasia con imitazione B m.; Praeludium and Fugato E m.; Praeludium et Fuga A m.; Praeludium (Rondo) F m.; Allegro *from Vivaldi Concerto G*; Fantasia con Fuga A m., Aria D (P-4510)

Air *on the G String* (D-280)

Andante *from fifth Flute Sonata.* Organ & Violin (P-3183)

Jesu, Man's Desire (N-728)

Siciliano *from second Flute Sonata* (D-752)

Toccata - Fantasia con Fuga in D (P-211a)

(b) *on three staves, in separate form:*

Christmas Oratorio: Pastoral Symphony (H. G. Ley) (P-38a)

Come, Holy Ghost, Facsimile reproduction of the 'Fantasia super Veni Sancte Spiritus,' with Portrait and Critical Analysis (Wackernagel) (De-117)

Concerto in D m. after Vivaldi ('*L'Estro Armonico*') (P-3002)

Concerto in A m. after Vivaldi (N-4036)

Fuga in E, from '48' (*The Saints in Glory*) (P-1c)

German Organ Mass *Clavieruebung*, Part III (P-3948)

Jesu, Man's Desire (P-264)

Magnificat. The Organ Part of the orchestral accompaniment (P-29b)

Passacaglia in C m. (N-4171)

Ricercar a 6 voci *from Musical Offering* (Hermann Keller) (P-4528)

Toccata and Fugue in D m. (P-261)

(c) *on three staves, in volume form:*

Album, containing Pastorale in F, Fugue in G à la Gigue, and Fugue in B m. on a theme of Corelli (H-355)

Art of Fugue. The complete work laid out for the Organ in an eminently practical manner (H. Schuricht):

   – Vol. 1 Contrapunctus I-XI (P-218i)

   – Vol. 2 Contrapunctus XII-XIX and Chorale (P-218k)

Articulation in Organ-Playing, including a 'Little Organ Book for Manuals only', based on 31 Chorale Preludes and Chorales by Bach in the order of the Liturgical Year (Gordon Phillips). With a Foreword by Robert Donington (H-1001)

Bach's Art of Part-Playing. A collection of six short Trios with advice on registration and method of study (S. de B. Taylor) (H-350k)

Bach's Method of Trio-Playing. The 2-part Inventions, arranged as trios for two manuals and pedal, the third part added by Max Reger and Karl Straube. No. De-709 (not for sale in U.S.A., Canada and Germany)

Musical Offering. The complete original edition with an Appendix containing (a) the Ricercare a 6 voci reduced to 2 or 3 staves for piano or organ, and (b) the Fuga Canonica arr. for Organ, or 2 or 3 players (P-219)

Orgelbuechlein Little Organ Books (P-3946)

Preludes, Fugues, Fantasias (P-4584)

Short Preludes and Fugues (eight) (P-4442)

(d) *Organ Vocal Score:*

Christmas Oratorio. The Vocal Parts, with Organ either as the sole accompaniment or together with such parts of a Full Orchestra as may be available. For use with all current 'Christmas Oratorio' editions, and playable on a moderate-sized 3- (or even 2-) manual organ, adapted by Marmaduke P. Conway and Robert S. Munns (P-7031a)

Date Due